Contents

KU-152-883

Weblink: www.science-at-school.com

Homes and schools work on electricity

Almost everything that works in a home or school runs on **BATTERIES** or uses mains supplies.

Look around your classroom or your home and you will discover that electricity is being used everywhere (Picture 1).

Electricity is an easy and controllable way of making things work. It is a source of **ENERGY**.

How electricity is used

In the home shown in Picture 1 you can see just a few of the things that are connected to mains electricity:
① fridge/freezer; ② ceiling lights;
③ computer; ④ desk fan; ⑤ room heaters.

▼ (Picture 1) Every room in our home has things that work with electricity.

4

There are, of course, many other things in a home that use electricity – electric cooker, toaster, kettle, iron, television, radio... the list is almost endless.

There are also things that use batteries for their electricity. They include: mobile phone; torch; pocket radio; portable CD player; TV remote control; smoke alarm; door bell.

Sources of electricity

As you will have noticed from the lists, there are two quite different ways we can get electricity for use.

One way is to use batteries. The other way is to use the electricity that comes from wall sockets. This is called **MAINS ELECTRICITY**.

Comparing mains and batteries

Things that work on the mains and things that run on batteries both use electricity.

Batteries are portable supplies and they are good for things that need to be carried around, but that do not need much electricity.

A mains supply is a shared supply of electricity. It delivers electricity equal to billions of batteries. It comes from a **POWER STATION** and is brought through **CABLES** to our homes (Picture 2). We then connect **APPLIANCES** to it by using plugs that we push into sockets in our walls.

Summary
- Batteries are used for small, portable pieces of equipment.
- Mains electricity is used for equipment needing a lot of power.
- Mains power comes from power stations.

▼ (Picture 2) The electricity we use at home or at school may come from a power station tens, or even hundreds, of kilometres away. It is carried through cables suspended on large towers (pylons) that carry it across the countryside. In cities, the cables are buried under the streets. Despite the huge size of a power station, the job it does is the same as a giant battery.

 Never touch mains sockets or bare wires connected to the mains.

Power station   Power lines

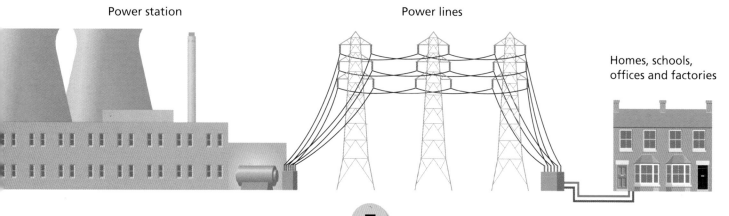

Homes, schools, offices and factories

Lighting and heating

We use mains power for things that need lots of electricity and which don't have to be moved about too much.

Lights, heaters, cookers, irons and washing machines all run on mains electricity.

Things work when electricity flows through them. Only certain materials allow electricity to flow through them. Most of these are metals, like copper and aluminium. So most of the things we use with electricity contain metals.

Lights

A light is one of the simplest things that uses electricity (Pictures 1, 2, 3 and 4). A light **BULB** contains a coil of very thin **WIRE** called a filament. It is special wire that won't melt when it gets hot. When the electricity flows in this wire, it glows very brightly and gives out light (and heat).

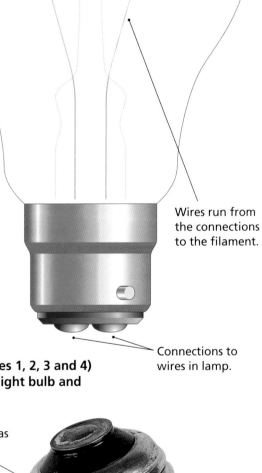

Filament heats up when light is switched on.

Glass bulb

Wires run from the connections to the filament.

Connections to wires in lamp.

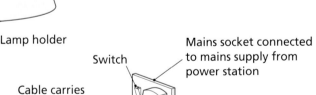

Light bulb

Lamp holder

Switch

Cable carries electricity

Mains socket connected to mains supply from power station

Plug

 (Pictures 1, 2, 3 and 4)
The parts of a light bulb and how it is used.

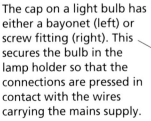

The cap on a light bulb has either a bayonet (left) or screw fitting (right). This secures the bulb in the lamp holder so that the connections are pressed in contact with the wires carrying the mains supply.

(Picture 5) This shows the heating element in a kettle.

Heaters

We use many kinds of heaters in the home (Pictures 5, 6 and 7). There are heaters in irons, in electric fires, in toasters, in electric showers and in electric kettles. They all work in the same way as a light bulb. Inside, there is a strip of wire called the element that gets hot when electricity flows through it. In a heater, the wire is thicker, because it takes more electrical **POWER** to heat things up quickly.

Summary
• Electricity can be used to produce light and heat.

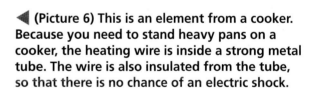

(Picture 6) This is an element from a cooker. Because you need to stand heavy pans on a cooker, the heating wire is inside a strong metal tube. The wire is also insulated from the tube, so that there is no chance of an electric shock.

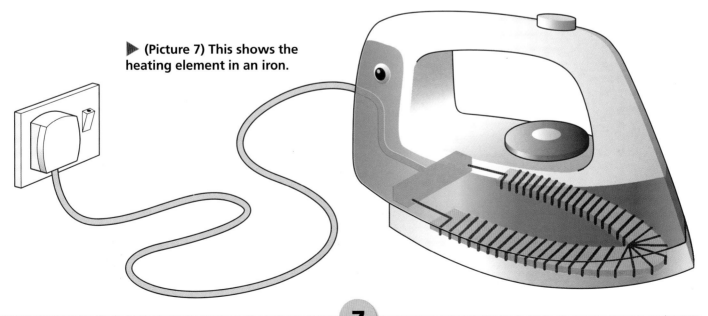

(Picture 7) This shows the heating element in an iron.

Weblink: www.science-at-school.com

Making a bulb light

To make a bulb light, you simply need to join the end of the bulb to each end of a battery.

You may think that it is hard to make electrical things. But as we have seen, if you take away the fancy cases, many electrical things are very simple. They are so simple, in fact, that we can make some battery-powered things with just a few items.

Metals carry electricity

It is important to remember that all metals allow electricity to flow through them. A material that does this is called a **CONDUCTOR**.

A material that doesn't allow electricity to flow through it is called an **INSULATOR**. Plastic and glass are insulators.

Now you can see why the equipment we looked at before was made mainly of plastic, glass and metal. The metal carried the electricity, while the glass and plastic protected us from it.

Make a connection

A connector is just a way of joining two things so electricity will be carried between them.

A wire is a connector. This has metal inside and plastic surrounding it. But for simple connections with a battery

you don't even need a wire – just a piece of aluminium kitchen foil.

The reason you can use kitchen foil is that any metal will carry electricity. Kitchen foil is made of aluminium, which is a metal, and so it will act as a conductor. If you cut a strip of aluminium foil and roll it up, it will even look like a wire.

▼▶ (Picture 1) All you need to make a bulb light.

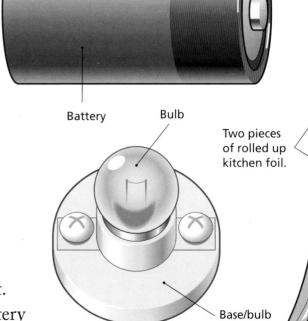

Battery

Bulb

Two pieces of rolled up kitchen foil.

Base/bulb holder

8

Weblink: www.science-at-school.com

Make it work

You need to get electricity to flow from one end, or **TERMINAL**, of the battery through the bulb and back to the other end of the battery. If you can make this happen, the bulb will light.

All you need is two pieces of rolled up kitchen foil, a battery, a bulb holder and a torch bulb (Picture 1).

You simply hold the foil strips against the ends of the battery, and then get someone else to touch the other ends of the foil strips against the connections of the bulb holder (Picture 2). Then the bulb will light. It's as simple as that.

Circuit

What you have done is to make a loop that electricity will flow through. It has a source of electricity (a battery), something you want to make work (a bulb) and a way of allowing electricity to flow between them (a conductor made of aluminium). This loop is called an electric **CIRCUIT**, and you have just made the simplest circuit.

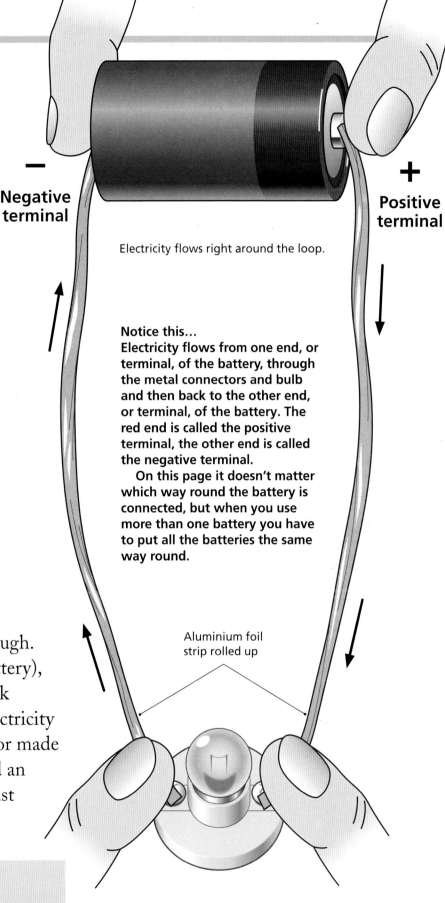

−

Negative terminal

+

Positive terminal

Electricity flows right around the loop.

Notice this…
Electricity flows from one end, or terminal, of the battery, through the metal connectors and bulb and then back to the other end, or terminal, of the battery. The red end is called the positive terminal, the other end is called the negative terminal.
On this page it doesn't matter which way round the battery is connected, but when you use more than one battery you have to put all the batteries the same way round.

Aluminium foil strip rolled up

▲ **(Picture 2) This diagram shows how to connect a battery to a bulb.**

Summary
- **Metals carry electricity.**
- **A loop carrying electricity is called a circuit.**
- **To make something work, electricity must flow out of one end of a battery and in to the other.**

Weblink: www.science-at-school.com

Using a circuit board

You cannot hold on to all the parts of a circuit all the time. But there is an easy way to keep everything in place.

The shape of the connectors in a circuit is not important. Professional electricians often arrange their connections in a tidy pattern so they can see what is going on.

A circuit board

A **CIRCUIT BOARD** is a board, on which sheets of metal are pasted to make a connection. Then items like bulbs and batteries are fastened to the board. This is the way all electrical equipment is held in place (Picture 1).

Make a circuit on a board

To make a circuit on a board, you need a sheet of aluminium foil, scissors, a piece of cardboard, some glue or wallpaper paste, some tape, a bulb and a battery (Picture 2).

Cut out the centre of the foil sheet. In this way you make a wide, square wire. The electricity must now flow around the edge of the board.

Stick the aluminium down with the glue or paste, and cut the foil where the battery and the bulb are to go. Lift up the strips of foil where you made the cuts.

Fasten the bulb and battery to the board with tape.

Now bring the aluminium foil tabs to the connectors of the bulb and the battery. You can hold them in place using tape.

The circuit is now complete and the bulb should light (Picture 3).

You can walk away and it will stay alight because it is all fixed in place.

▼ (Picture 1) Part of a circuit board for a radio.

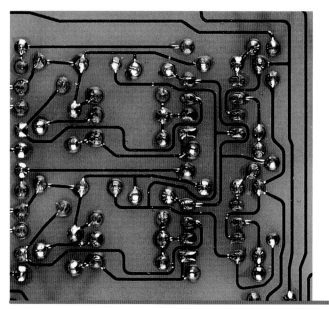

▶ (Picture 2) What you need to make a circuit board.

Summary
• A circuit board keeps the connections nicely organised and reduces the chance of a mistake.

Weblink: www.science-at-school.com

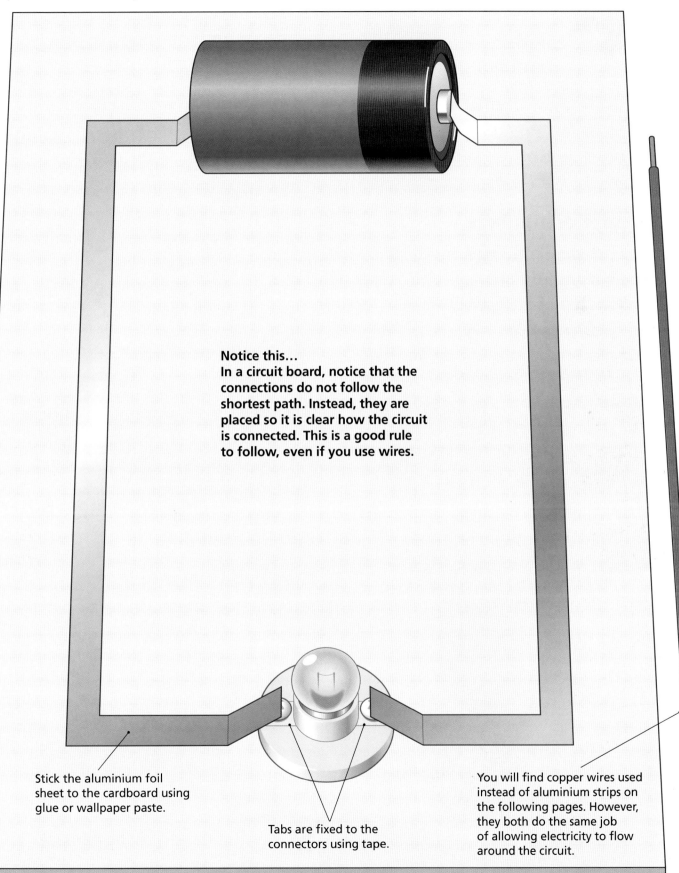

Notice this…
In a circuit board, notice that the connections do not follow the shortest path. Instead, they are placed so it is clear how the circuit is connected. This is a good rule to follow, even if you use wires.

Stick the aluminium foil sheet to the cardboard using glue or wallpaper paste.

Tabs are fixed to the connectors using tape.

You will find copper wires used instead of aluminium strips on the following pages. However, they both do the same job of allowing electricity to flow around the circuit.

11

Matching batteries to a bulb

The pressure, or voltage, in the battery must be matched to the voltage of the bulb if the bulb is to shine brightly and not burn out.

Now that we have seen how a circuit connects **COMPONENTS** together, we must look a little more carefully at matching the bulb to the battery.

Looking for numbers

Batteries make electricity from chemicals. We can't change the amount of electricity that comes out of the battery. Each battery delivers a **VOLTAGE**, or electrical pressure, of one and a half volts (1.5V). You will find this printed on the side of the battery.

You have to match this number with the number on the bulb you are using. Look for the number on the side of the bulb (Picture 1).

Matching the numbers

How do you know how many batteries to use with the bulb? The answer is easy.

If a bulb has 3 volts (3V) stamped on the side, then you match this by putting two batteries in line. Remember: Batteries are 1.5 volts each and if you add 1.5 to 1.5 you get 3 (1.5 + 1.5 = 3). This is shown in Picture 2.

If you add too little

Suppose you put in too few batteries? Then there won't be enough electrical pressure to drive the electricity around the circuit and the bulb will be dim (Picture 3). However, if you are not sure what to do, adding fewer batteries is the safe option.

Don't add too much

If you add more batteries than the bulb makers intended, then the electrical pressure will be too high. The bulb will have too much electricity flowing through it and this will make the wire inside (the filament) too hot. It will produce a very bright light for a short while and then burn out (Picture 4).

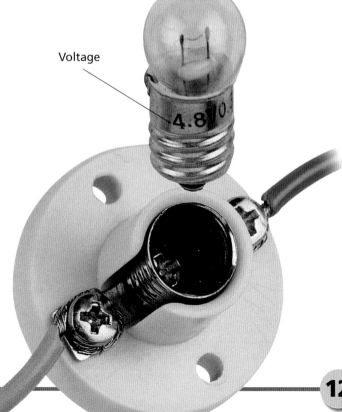

Voltage

4.8

(Picture 1) Look for the correct operating voltage on the side of the bulb.

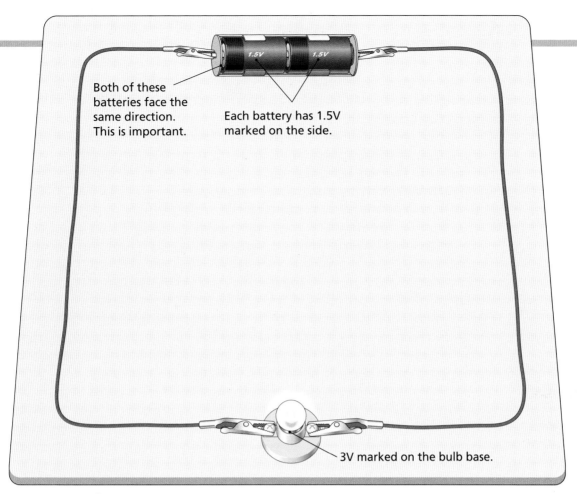

Both of these batteries face the same direction. This is important.

Each battery has 1.5V marked on the side.

3V marked on the bulb base.

⚠ (Picture 2) Two batteries and a 3V bulb give the correct light.

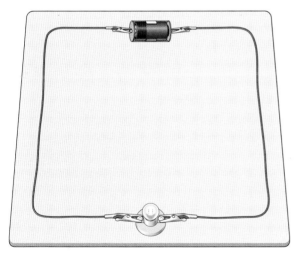

⚠ (Picture 3) Here, using just one battery results in a dim light.

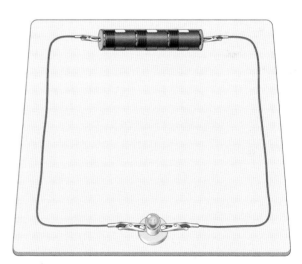

⚠ (Picture 4) Three batteries and only one bulb will cause the bulb to burn out.

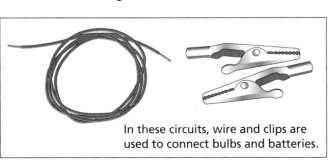

In these circuits, wire and clips are used to connect bulbs and batteries.

Summary
- Match the number of batteries to the amount of voltage the bulb needs.
- Too few batteries and the bulb will be too dim.
- Too many batteries and the bulb will burn out.

Weblink: www.science-at-school.com

Switches

Switches are used to break the circuit and control the flow of electricity.

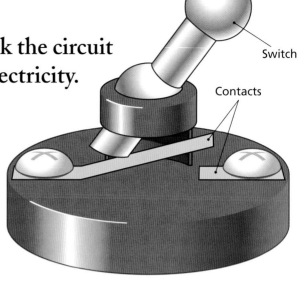

Switch

Contacts

Electricity flows when all the parts of a circuit make a loop. Electricity flows from one end, or terminal, of the battery, through the wires, bulbs, and whatever else is connected, and then back to the other end, or terminal, of the battery (Picture 1).

The current flows because every part is joined in a loop. If one part of the circuit is not joined to the next, no current flows and the circuit does not work.

This is not always a bad thing. For example, we may not want to leave a light bulb on all the time, because then the battery will soon be worn out.

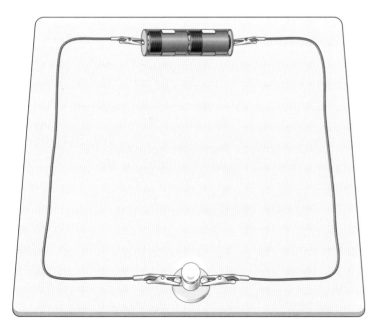

▲ **(Picture 1) There is no easy way of controlling the way electricity flows in this circuit.**

▲ **(Picture 2) A switch has two contacts that are pushed together when the switch is on. They spring apart when the switch is off.**

The switch

To stop the flow of electricity, you need to break the circuit. You could simply pull the wires off the bulb or the battery, but this is a slow and awkward method, and the wires would soon get broken.

A **SWITCH** is a small device that reliably breaks and remakes the circuit. The switch in Picture 2 contains two springy metal plates called contacts. When the switch is turned off (opened), the contacts spring apart.

You can see how a switch controls a circuit in Pictures 3 and 4. When the switch is off, the contacts spring apart and the bulb goes off (Picture 3); when the switch is turned on (closed), the contacts are pushed together and the bulb lights up (Picture 4).

Summary
• A switch is used to control the flow of electricity.

Weblink: www.science-at-school.com

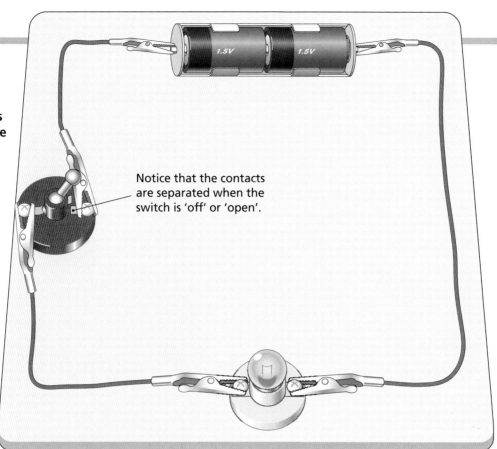

(Picture 3)
A circuit with a switch in it looks like this. Here the switch is off.

Notice that the contacts are separated when the switch is 'off' or 'open'.

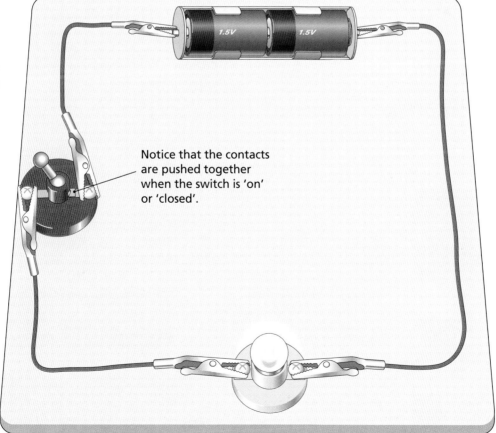

(Picture 4)
Now the switch is at the 'on' position. Notice the contacts are closed.

Notice that the contacts are pushed together when the switch is 'on' or 'closed'.

15

How a torch works

A torch uses a circuit and all of the components we have seen so far.

On pages 14 and 15, you saw how a circuit was made using batteries, bulb and switch. This circuit is shown again here in Picture 1.

This is the circuit used in a very useful piece of equipment – the torch.

However, the circuit does not make a very useful torch when placed on a board. To be useful, the circuit must be carefully fitted into a case.

Choosing batteries

There are many sizes of torch. Why is this? Mostly because different torches use different sizes and different numbers of batteries.

The bigger the battery, the more **POWER** it gives out and the longer it lasts (Picture 2). But you can get long-lasting batteries in each size, too (Picture 3).

▼ (Picture 1) A circuit that can be used to make a torch.

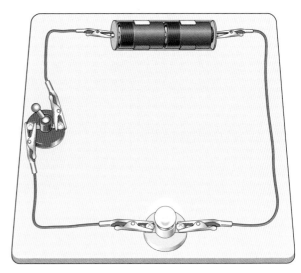

Two, four and even six batteries used in a line are common in torches. The batteries must all be placed in the case facing the same direction. In general, the more batteries, the bigger the voltage and the more powerful the bulb can be.

▼ (Picture 3) These batteries are the same voltage and the same size, but the one on the top lasts longer than the one on the bottom. It is more expensive to buy, but because it lasts longer, it is cheaper to run. It lasts longer because it has different chemicals packed inside it.

◄ (Picture 2) These batteries all have the same voltage, but they have different amounts of chemicals packed inside them. The bigger the battery, the longer it will last.

Weblink: www.science-at-school.com

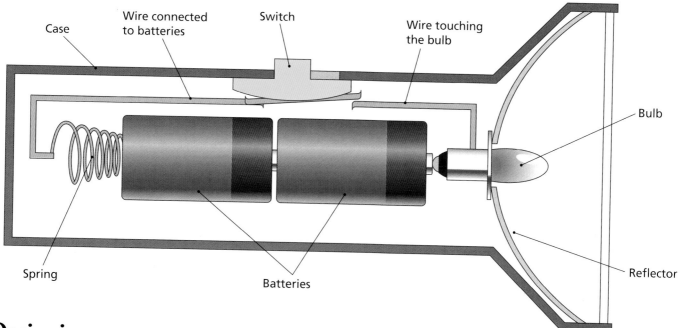

Case — Wire connected to batteries — Switch — Wire touching the bulb — Bulb — Spring — Batteries — Reflector

Designing a case

The torch is made in the shape of a tube because a tube is convenient to carry (Pictures 4 and 5). But happily, a tube is also the same shape as the batteries.

The circuit in a torch could be broken accidentally as the torch is carried around. To prevent this, a spring is used to hold the batteries against the bulb. Notice that the spring is metal and is also used as one of the connections to the switch. The bulb is held in front of a shiny dish, the reflector, to make the beam shine forwards.

The circuit is completed when the switch is pushed – connecting the wire leading from the batteries to the wire touching the bulb.

▼ (Picture 5) These are all the pieces that go into a torch.

Summary
• Torches are simple circuits in a cleverly designed case.
• Some batteries last longer than others.
• Torches with more batteries have more powerful bulbs.
• Batteries must be fitted the right way round.

Weblink: www.science-at-school.com

Circuits that will and will not work

A circuit only works when it makes a loop.

Electricity must flow in a loop. The shape of the loop and the length of the loop do not matter much (Picture 1). But, the loop must start at one end of a battery and finish at the other end. The things you want to make work must be fitted into this loop.

What you notice in Picture 1 is that long loops can be tangled and difficult to follow. This is why complicated circuits are often put on to circuit boards.

▼ (Picture 1) The length and shape of the connector are not important. All of these circuits work exactly the same way.

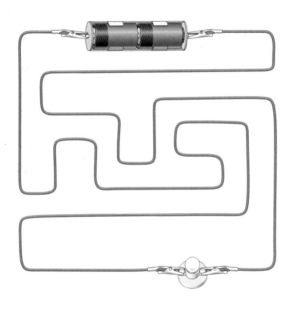

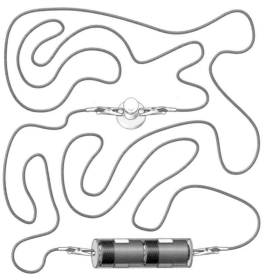

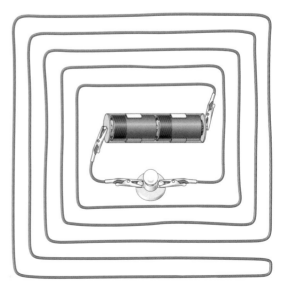

Weblink: www.science-at-school.com

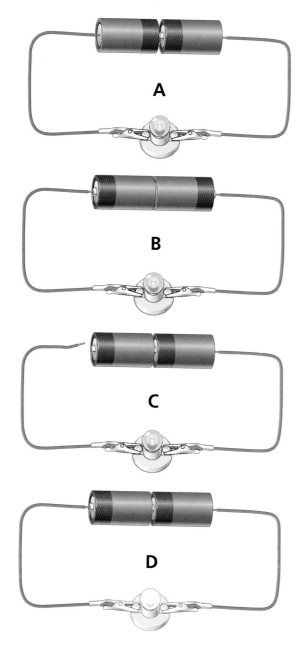

Circuits that won't work

The rules for making a circuit work are simple, but very strict. The rules also include the batteries. Picture 2A shows you a circuit that won't work because the batteries are placed facing one another. Picture 2B shows a circuit that won't work because the batteries are placed facing away from one another. Picture 2C shows a circuit that won't work because a wire is not connected. To work, the batteries must always face in the same direction and all wires must be connected (Picture 2D).

A loop must start from one end of a battery and finish at the other end. Picture 3A shows a circuit with the connectors both starting from the same end. This won't work. The correct circuit is shown in Picture 3B.

▲ (Picture 2) Circuits A, B and C will not work. The correct circuit is D.

Summary
- Circuits only work when the connections all form a loop from one end of the battery to the other.
- Circuits only work if good connections are made between components.

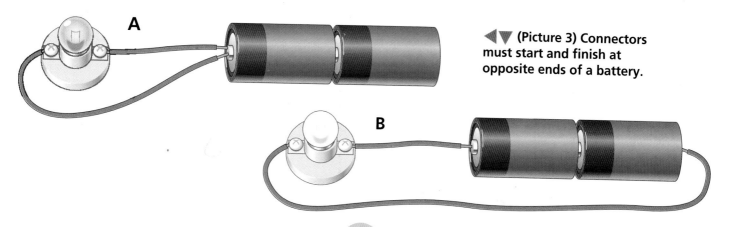

◀▼ (Picture 3) Connectors must start and finish at opposite ends of a battery.

Weblink: www.science-at-school.com

Adding to the loop

You can have as many bulbs in a circuit as you like. You just need to match them to the batteries.

When you connect up electrical equipment using a single loop, you are making a **SERIES CIRCUIT** (Picture 1).

In a series circuit, the same amount of electricity flows through each bulb, and so they all glow with the same brightness. If there are too few batteries or too many bulbs, all the lights are dim. The electricity is NOT all used up by the first bulb, leaving nothing for the next.

Instead, the bulbs have to share the electricity, so there is not enough electricity to light up the bulbs brightly.

Adding bulbs

Picture 1 shows two batteries connected in a loop to a switch and two light bulbs. Notice that both of the light bulbs form part of a single loop.

If you were to make this circuit and switch it on, you would find the bulbs shine with a dimmer light than if the circuit had just one bulb.

This shows that, the more bulbs (or any other components) you have strung together in a line (in series), the more batteries are needed to keep the items working at full strength.

▼ **(Picture 1) This is a series circuit with two bulbs (3V + 3V = 6V) in a continuous loop with two batteries (1.5V + 1.5V = 3V). The voltages do not match, so the bulbs are dim.**

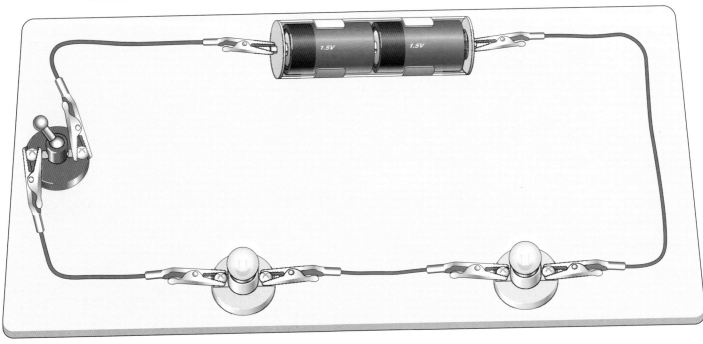

Weblink: www.science-at-school.com

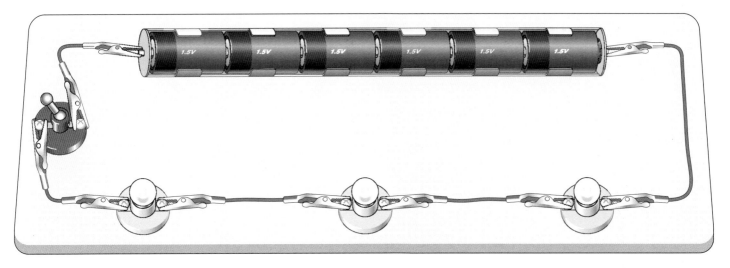

▲ (Picture 2) A series circuit with six 1.5V batteries (1.5 + 1.5 + 1.5 + 1.5 + 1.5 + 1.5 = 9V) and three 3V bulbs (3 + 3 + 3 = 9V). The sum of the voltages match, so the bulbs will shine brightly.

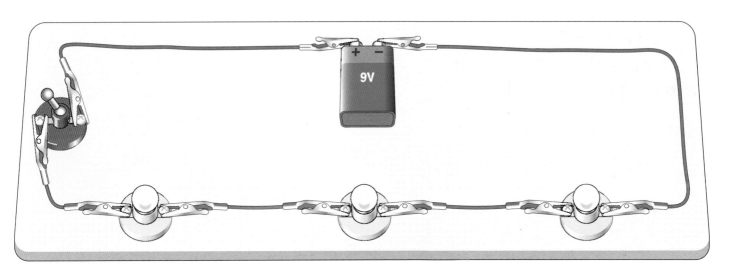

▲ (Picture 3) How does this work? There are three bulbs and only one battery? The answer is that the battery says 9V on the side!

Matching batteries to bulbs

To get a bright light, you have to make sure that the sum of all the numbers on the bulbs is the same as the sum of all the numbers on the batteries.

This is shown in Pictures 2 and 3.

As you can see, when there are lots of bulbs in a series circuit, lots of voltage is needed.

Summary
• A circuit will work best if the sum of the voltage numbers on the batteries matches the sum of the voltage numbers on the bulb.

Weblink: www.science-at-school.com

Testing for conductors and insulators

Electricity can only flow through some materials. These are called conductors.

We may take it for granted that electricity flows in a wire. But why doesn't it spill out of the wire and flow through the air, or through ourselves?

The answer is that electricity can only travel through certain substances.

Conductors

Metals are the most commonly used conductors. Most of the wires you will use to make circuits contain many thin strands of copper twisted together (Picture 1).

Many liquids are also conductors. Salty water and the water in our taps and rivers are conductors. As a result, touching electrical things with wet hands can make you part of an electrical circuit – and this can be very dangerous.

Insulators

Materials that do not let electricity pass through them are called electrical insulators. Plastics are insulators. They are used, for example, as a sleeve around wires (Picture 1), on switches and as plugs. Air is another good insulator.

▼ (Picture 1) These three wires all contain twisted strands of copper, which is a good conductor. The coloured sleeves are made of plastic because it is a good insulator.

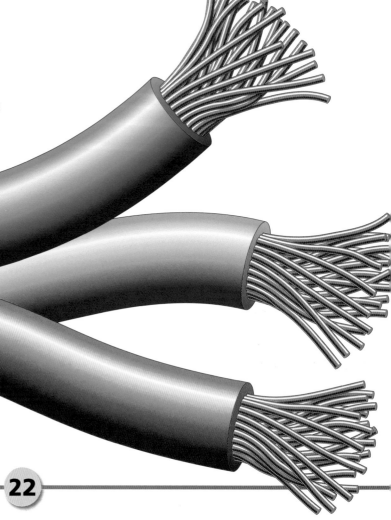

⚠ (Picture 2) In this picture, a metal spoon is being tested. The bulb lights up, proving that the metal spoon is a conductor.

Conductor or insulator?

One way to find out which materials are insulators and which are conductors is to make a loop (electrical circuit) using the same circuit we have used throughout this book (Picture 2). If the object being tested is a conductor, the electricity will flow through the whole circuit and the bulb will light up. If the object is an insulator, the electricity cannot flow around the circuit and the bulb will not light up.

Summary

• Electricity will only flow through a conductor and will not flow through an insulator.

Weblink: www.science-at-school.com

Index

Science@School

Science@School is a series published by Atlantic Europe Publishing Company Ltd.

Atlantic Europe Publishing

Teacher's Guide
There is a Teacher's Guide with activity and comprehension worksheets to accompany this book.

CD-ROMs
There are some browser-based CD-ROMs containing information to support the Science@School series.

Dedicated Web Site
There's more information about other great Science@School packs and a wealth of supporting material available at our dedicated web site:

www.science-at-school.com

First published in 2001 by
Atlantic Europe Publishing Company Ltd

Copyright © 2001
Atlantic Europe Publishing Company Ltd
Reprinted 2005

All rights reserved. No part of this publication may be reproduced, stored in a retrieval system, or transmitted in any form or by any means, electronic, mechanical, photocopying, recording or otherwise, without prior permission of the publisher.

Author
Brian Knapp, BSc, PhD

Educational Consultant
Peter Riley, BSc

Art Director
Duncan McCrae, BSc

Senior Designer
Adele Humphries, BA, PGCE

Editor
Lisa Magloff, BA

Illustrations
David Woodroffe

Designed and produced by
Earthscape Editions

Reproduced in Malaysia by
Global Colour

Printed in China by
WKT Co., Ltd

Science@School
Volume 4F *Simple electricity*
A CIP record for this book is available from the British Library.

Paperback ISBN 1 86214 144 4

Picture credits
All photographs are from the Earthscape Editions photolibrary.

This product is manufactured from sustainable managed forests. For every tree cut down at least one more is planted.

24